GRAVITATION

PITT POETRY SERIES

Nancy Krygowski and Jeffrey McDaniel, *Editors*

GRAVITATION

SELECTED POEMS

MILAN DĚŽINSKÝ

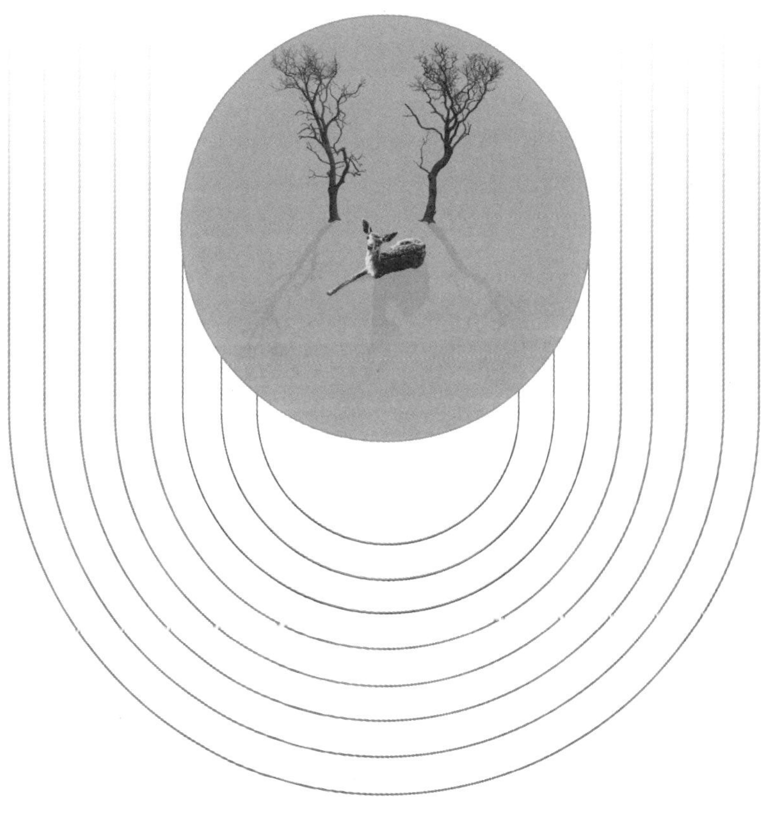

TRANSLATED BY NATHAN FIELDS

Published by the University of Pittsburgh Press, Pittsburgh, Pa., 15260

Manufactured in the United States of America

Printed on acid-free paper

10 9 8 7 6 5 4 3 2 1

ISBN 13: 978-0-8229-6769-9

ISBN 10: 0-8229-6769-3

Cover art and design by Alex Wolfe

Book design by Alex Wolfe

Publisher: University of Pittsburgh Press, 7500 Thomas Blvd., 4th floor, Pittsburgh, PA 15260, United States, www.upittpress.org

EU Authorized Representative: Easy Access System Europe, Mustamäe tee 50, 10621 Tallinn, Estonia, gpsr.requests@easproject.com

CONTENTS

FROM *A SECRET LIFE* (2012)

FROM *WALKING AROUND AN ISLAND* (2017)

FROM *THE SIXTH FINGER* (2022)

GRAVITATION

FROM *A SECRET LIFE* (2012)

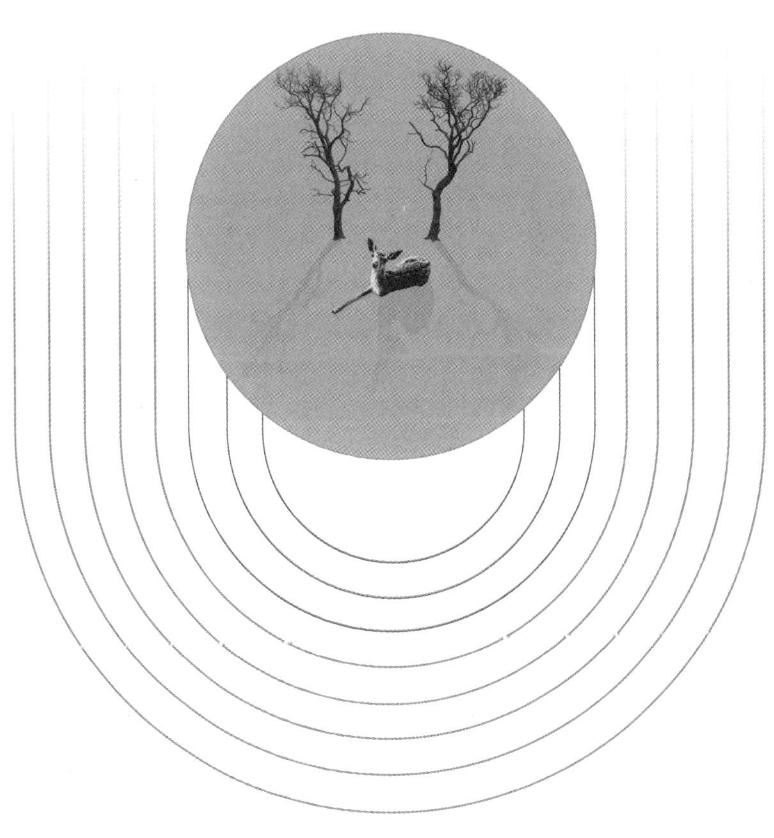

ATOM

It is sixty-five years since Hiroshima,
they write. Should one cup a handful of water from a river,
there is certainly in it at least one atom of oxygen
that Cleopatra exhaled, I have read,
or was it Marilyn?
I hear my daughter's sobbing
through the wall, in whose marlstone joints
still trembles a tear of builder's sweat.
The house is secreting saliva from the bedrock.
When she struggled her way into the world,
I paced the room.
Had she been given a gift
of one atom from Hiroshima?

BUZZARD

I had taken him to his mother
and was returning along the D8.
In the emergency lane several cars, and behind them
scattered papers like a snail's trail.
I thought about how many things
it is possible to learn: to speak again, to use your legs
instead of your hands, to let yourself, like a newt,
grow joy inside your body,
tissue to tissue, joyfully linked cells.
Like a table cleared with a sleeve, the empty highway
signaled that the healing time
would be written with a tiny pinkish scar
into the calendar of memory.

And then—I saw it out of the corner of my eye,
like someone indicating an attack
and a shadow passed perilously
like a startled doe—
a falling buzzard, rotating, like when a plane's engine
cuts out, and then crashes
into the azure highway
somewhere far behind the car.
I imagine that disheveled remnant,
collapsed into itself upon the merciless surface,
as if it still didn't know how to fly,

chilled in her meager nest
and she watched that blue above her,
predatory head adamantly lodged
between two wings whose tips
are ruffled by the breeze like a promise . . .
I watch behind me as her bird body
calms in quivers, the wind ruffling her again
as it slowly dissolves
like sleep.

GRAVITATION

They're having a picnic, but it looks as
if they were taking the tools out of the car in an emergency,
or they are taking the tools out of the car,
but it looks as if they were going out on a picnic.
A body does not thrust itself against the floor of an elevator,
but the elevator against the body.
Dusk does not fall upon the city,
the city slides creeping in beneath the dusk.
A hawk does not propel itself toward a mouse,
the mouse catapults itself against the predator.
At the opposite bank a barge rolls the river under itself.
We are not approaching our end,
but from ultimate emptiness
the end is hurtling toward us.

WHAT TO SAY ABOUT A WORLD

that stands out where it's not smooth.
To disappear in the fields and never return.
Let a messenger ring
and not leave a message.
To walk out to the edge of the forest.
Change into a tree in front of mushroom pickers,
and stick out oddly in the shade, so that they notice,
with a root knotting the footpath.
Be whipped like a dog rough with a rope.
Let the boy rustle the branch with a stick.
Be the resting place
of a sparrowhawk zeroing in on a dove.
Stand bare against Alpine wind,
have in your bast an ingrown message
that remained undelivered.

NOVEMBER

Such a picture of withering
demands active engagement.
Chrysanthemums bloom into the snow
like the color of a wounded animal.
A free moment between increments
of time filled with decay.
The mathematical beauty of frost.
Structures organize.
The end of struggling through mud.
At the end of November the plum tree
smells like dog kibble.
We sit and watch the chickadees in the feeder,
drinking hot tea, a celebration of security
with dusk's familiar arrival.
Who wouldn't love the gray Sunday afternoon;
we're already so far from the scene with the fox
dragging its injured spine along the highway
like stolen prey.

INTO THE DARKNESS

Return to the darkness, Ranchetti calls out
from one of his poems, as if he were still wavering,
to see whether there were another way. But there's not
from the moment we were
waterlilies in the womb and wrenched
by a random, undesired gust.
And so it goes on.
We unconsciously search for an outlet
or a gullet, depending on whether it's just
getting rid of us, or swallowing us;
we wake in the night,
when in our sleep we're frightened by a deer,
with steam rising from its back,
which is getting up out of the snow heavily
on three legs.

TOMATOES

Yellow and rusty layer of leaves
peel like old skin,
light sprays along houses, cars, fences
pours over a grayish face in the window—it's me,
life behind me, another life before it
in a series of small movements.
This moment is only a delay:
tomatoes,
waiting blankly at the executioner's block,
on the verge of exploding and sourly burning
the impression of morning, scorch the light,
burn the face.
Victorious tomatoes.

AMONG DEBRIS

Every secluded corner will one day be a square in the metropolis.
All life will be discovered and all death clarified.
Hills and forests will be disassembled in the dark of night
and placed into boxes and reassembled just before dawn
and arranged along the highways.
The calm before the storm will become the storm before the endless calm,
from which you will poke things through a slot to the other side
there, where you lived.

LOVERS

As if they were trying to pull each other down
under the sharp edge of the waterline, where voracious demons
stretch out their hands from their underwater empire.
And having the upper hand. Pushing him below you:
the fierceness of bones, the voracity of membranes. One emerges:
using his last strength to breathe, a tuft of hair devours his palm,
leveraging with a knee. Buttocks beating with the heart of a horse.
So as in times long ago, even today
passionate, deadly aggressors. And when everything is over,
the shudder slowly fades in the pectoral girdle.
The heart is quiet. They are each alone.

JIGSAW

I stop at the wall of the moist forest:

A log drowns in mud like a deer halfway up to its chest.
Silence buzzes after crickets.
The extinguished star of a snail shell
whose light swallows me
and then spits me out a bit further.

At the footpath a jigsaw.
Two birds' scattered skeletons
mingled in one last turtledove kiss.

They will lie there, I imagine,
in that beautiful forest,
in rain, in heat,
chill,

till new birth
does them part.

ORDERLY EXISTENCE

A tree rots in the forest unnoticed.
Lichen trims bark. A raucous reek.
The bruised framework sinks into the earth.
A woman with a man's physique treads the path sobbing.
The night telephone above the table takes a bite out of
the darkness.
A dog that begins to howl in its sleep,
as if it weren't supposed to be alive anymore.
Power over words is power over things.
We sleep and have everything—relations,
a favorite restaurant, happy home.
But something here's not clicking. Not only words.

I'LL BE THIRTY-THREE

They leave me alone
and while the kettle clucks like a hen,
I realize that at my age
Ginsberg and Corso had long written
the most beautiful poems:
about a girl from Park Avenue,
about thought, which is all
the poet knows of death.
Even I am sometimes seized by an itch
that cannot be relieved until one
slumps down into transformation,
as if an ugly flower were struggling up out of one's chest
and *someone else* were plucking the petals,
but it was as if they were tearing out a wart,
something revoltingly yours,
penetrated by fate,
veined with spongy tissue,
expressing itself with sweat,
which is a manifestation of craving
but also of openness
when I address myself in a whisper
here at this lamp, here in this darkness—

SPRING

Benumbed bees on partially open
blossoms like detaching fingernails.
Bracket fungus dusts the spring moisture
like musty flour.
The observant face of Theodore Roethke
hatches in a chicken wrinkle.
The air smells of memory.
A grub beneath a sandal
digs a black hole in a parallel universe.
Jolting its translucent core.
The past has found a crevice, the world rejoices.
Just before noon
a plow dislocates a rat head from the soil.

WAKING UP

All I know is that this is waking up.
Warmed by a trickle of water in the gutter,
leaning against the membrane of a throbbing vein. Black force
rises up. I'm searching still half-blind
for a shaken-off shoe.
The dark places where I feel good hold me by a handle of bone.
Dreams slipping like clothes out of a hotel closet
are flowing into my awakening
like blood into a wound.
I perceive a mere melody of thoughts.
But now I'm starting to look around.
I finally see my benevolent room,
I feel the damp bed
and monstrous banality.

BURNING THE BRANCHES

After winter my loved ones burn branches.
Children listlessly suck dead-nettle flowers.
The sweetness saturates this day in May.
Reeds are burning. With a cry a blackbird chick
flits away from a dog.
An insect melts above the fire.
A lizard is a twisted, rusty wire.
Birch above the flames flutters and raises dust like a broom.
A hedgehog flees, on his back a burn-fused scab
of spikes. We look into the fire,
as if again witnessing
the creation of the world.

TUAREG

Based on the experience of Z. Štolovský

People on the street
emerge unaware like divers.

When two Tuareg meet, however,
they come alive and already start greeting each other from a great distance.
When they meet face to face, they rub palm against palm,
they ask about family, sheep, camels,
neglecting nothing.

Great, fanning gesture.

When they part, they wish a safe journey,
and as they gradually move away from one another,
they still chat a little,
like when there's a bit of tea left at the bottom.

Then, slowly shrinking,
they quiver and fade against the horizon,
like a well being filled.

A SECRET LIFE

The thought that a secret life really exists
is terrifying. Shadows would dress for the night
and set out into the rain. While sleepers are experiencing dreams,
they steal off toward the lamps stark naked under coats.
But maybe it's just part of the plan—
all those cloaking maneuvers, obligations, stupor and sex,
for a secret life can only be played out in sharp light.
We have but unreliable evidence: a bitten nail,
strangely colored flakes of skin, a fragment of a poem on a wall.
An unseeing vein bit its way through a muscle.
Very bright side light colliding with muffled music
is like flushing.
A forgotten or exchanged object. A watch in the fridge among the eggs.
Or—
The secret life is the visible part—property issues,
getting up for work, parental effort, the need to share,
grueling weekend fun.

HUNTER

I.

The power,
when a poem is not created, but comes into being,
when it settles in grooves like a tree ring in the furniture,
it creaks and in its quivering disturbs
the peace of the dust.
Like a hunter, I wait for this moment
rubbing a numbed leg.
Spring dawns above the wing of the forest,
the hunter cools his cheek against the gun barrel,
which will, any moment,
certainly turn into an antler.

II.

I have a metaphor in mind,
large and complicated,
when from my morning bowl of muesli
I clumsily fish out a precious
hazelnut,
it's burrowing all the way to the bottom.
I, vigilant hunter,
will find it in the end.
That effort is rewarded with delight,
though what's left is a lot of muesli
without hazelnuts.

1985

When she ironed,
it smelled of starch and canvas,
in the choral of that aroma Sunday stiffened,
tidying was done, and when someone said war, they meant
that war . . .
but the wall seems impossible to scale only when we are a step
away from it, the wall . . . But we didn't often think about the war.
On Sunday we watched
ski jumping on TV.

CELEBRATION

When I spotted the dead guy I felt like when
they bring you in and take the blindfold off your eyes.
Today I recall his glossy face.
Funereal guests, serious and aware of the moment,
bow over the styrofoam complexion
and over clasped palms, like when you knead to gray
all the clay. The room is dark;
light inspires unceremonious thoughts.
Mourning is an orderly expression of grieving.
They watch slightly askance so as not to be struck by the discharge
of some kind of posthumous prescience that might flare up out of the matter.
The dead guy had been carefully groomed and prepared.
I only wondered at how still he lay there
in view of the seriousness of the celebration.

* * *

Based on the poems of John Donne and Allen Ginsberg

It so happens that before you fall even deeper
below the rustling thirst of leaves, loose soil,
through the chasm of memory before awakening,
you will fall in like a puzzle piece
among the mingled bones of lovers,
between his fragile metatarsals
and her white femur.
Taut in frozen horror,
witness to their endless intercourse,
you won't move, for fear of being caught.

SIEVE

They attentively sifted their whole life through a sieve.
They believed something would remain and not fall through,
but their names will fade,
the sun whitens them, the wind grinds, the rain washes away,
neither in memories, nor on damp paper,
and I know, not even in poems,
let alone in poems.

STATE OF WAR

In the uncovered slope of overturned layers,
like when a foot is long stifled in a tight shoe:
A concertina of Carboniferous, Triassic, Permian—shuffled cards.
The dull stone skull of a cynodont juts from one of them.
Beside the tracks above the river, swans have armed explosives
under their wings.
You reach an end that disappears like a flare in a gun barrel.
In the blackness men buried beneath a mound
of snoring. You look back nervously under covering fire.
In a window, beside a flowerpot,
someone has set a celery's fuse.

TV STAR

The smooth armpit of a TV star
explodes bluely in a solitude of darkness
and you're stuck, eaten
like a shoe caught between two
continents sliding
against each other,
you crumble with the mobility of a clod,
like when you saw those lovers' hands
in the shopping center,
two hot, collapsing,
centripetal universes
curved
toward good moments
and the unrepeatable
shabbiness of the day.

HALLEY'S COMET

No revolution is in progress,
it's just our mysterious future
creeping in from somewhere.
It emerges from an archeology of shadows
and taps in time.
Through the wall I hear an old woman
welcoming a squeaking door.
She looks down the street
like through a telescope,
but sees only the back of a stranger.
She knows what's not awaiting her,
but has no clue what awaits her.
When Halley's Comet
flies over, we'll be together.
Struggling up out of the soil,
changing into leaves,
golden pollen will whirl
branches will be bent
so she can see it.

MOLLUSK SHELLS

As if in an endeavor
to leave something here,
but I don't have in mind kilos of soft tissue.
It's as if I were in a wormhole:
I change the channel and see that same face,
just cast roughly by time:
young Annie from Trautenberk
and the schoolteacher from better times,
all those black-and-white fairy tales
full of the living dead.
It's like a collection of mollusk shells
rattling in a shoebox.
Is life long or short?
There are plenty of other things
to think about,
what to eat and what to wear,
dispelling feelings of loneliness,
there even remains a moment for compassion,
love, and white lies.
Someday everything will rattle
in another box.

CUTTING

Cutting into bread, defiant in its acquiescence.
Cutting into a pepper crunches menacingly like the bolt of a rifle.
Cutting into a potato with a starchy stutter,
like when a zipper starts to open and the line of the cut fills with blue.
A careless slit in a wooden tabletop is a wrinkle.
Cutting inspiring a thought or movement.
The mechanical cutting into a rabbit to remove its head
holds grace in the snap of the spine.
The sharp cutting into a mushroom, smooth as butter cake,
strikes the whole forest.

ACCESSORY

I wouldn't be able to love her.
Just the suspicion of that giant tongue . . .
But when she spoke she skillfully concealed it within the hollow
from which darkness spews.
Crimson, dully shining accessory of mortality.
But I knew it was there, filling her entirely,
that perhaps as a living muscle it had devoured
the space of her body along with her organs. A fleshy slithering parasite.
Although everything was forcing me to believe it was only my
overactive imagination, I knew it was there.

FROM *WALKING AROUND AN ISLAND* (2017)

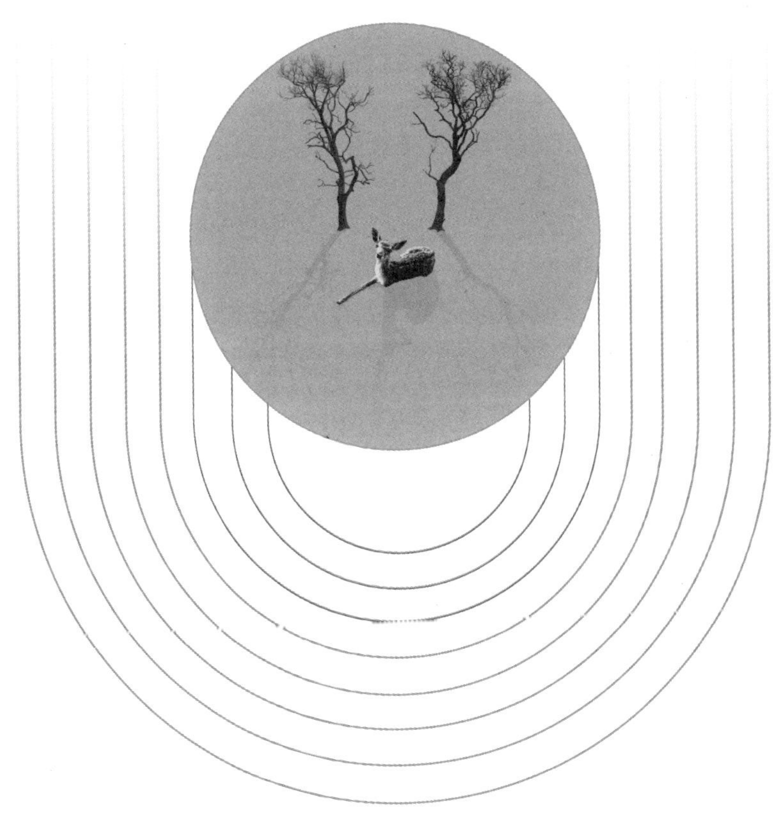

HAPPINESS

For those looking from the train we look like pure happiness.
But happiness can make you lose hair.

We are walking to the sand pit with the last dog.
The bicycles are of fragile construction.
When a train passes, the younger child smiles.
Those watching don't see the dead little bird,
the butterfly dying from exhaustion.
The children see them.

Tell me, sincere observer,
what thing is growing in my stomach and what should I do with it?

FROM THE SHORE

Whoever has burned down once, won't burst into flames.
I don't travel.
I have a table, an island, I've carved a river into it with an upturned trunk:

shouts come from its shores and that is poetry.

Poems about cottages in a garden colony
or poems like a revolutionary banner with sobs fraying at its edges.

I most like those that speak plainly about complex things,
and then those that speak simply about simple things.

To live for a hundred years and only die for a day.
Crawl up to the peak and then slide down it,

fall like a worn-out sandal.

There's a strange wind blowing today, my back is slack.

In its beak a seagull carries a poem that is trembling
and there's a fin sticking out of it red as a cherry.

ABOUT A COMET

A boy timidly waves and the train departs.
I think about today, what makes it different?
Maybe that I read about a comet.

Sometimes a comet doesn't return.

A backpack carries off a schoolgirl like a colorful bird of prey.
Two abandoned bags with ears perked in the station hall.
Behind foggy windows girls send each other smoke signals.

You can see the brewery from here,
a boat mooring at the dock.
People from the desert carry shyness into the hall.

You almost can't see them through the station
window: Two pagan goddesses—
one coughing fire into the face of the other.

DAY

Crammed in the car with a frantic dog in the trunk,
we bore the autumn sun upon the hood
and looked for a hill where the wind was blowing.

Someone strict had ordered it away.

The children stood around the field with kites like faded flags.
The wind didn't pick up until we'd gotten home.
It was a day in vain, but we'll remember it.

AFTER A CAR CRASH

The car floated up and flew through the snow-laden trees.
Later that night when I was coming back by train from that place,
whose name I first heard over the telephone,
I pressed my wet feet to the heating, in which dust was being burned.

Flakes were borne onto the deserted train station and decommissioned cisterns.
Darkness and lost, scattered light that pressed inside the stomach
were interrupted by the deafening express train to Turnov like a fiery hand
and in the last window a phantom, tearing off its face.

IF A TRAIN . . .

If a train leaves the station with constant acceleration
until it achieves a speed of 140 km/h,
and from the opposite direction a commuter train approaches from Hněvice
decelerating to zero,
at which speed will both trains move away from the convex shadow
of an animal in a birch grove
hit by the cross-fire of their tail lights
in the event that a tired passenger with a scuffed suitcase
reaches for the handle of the station toilet
and the door is locked?

BOAT ON A LAKE

We talk about rules,
and while I read you a poem, the door opens.

There's nothing behind it, just an endless lake.

Upon it bobs a red and blue boat
from the time of the ancient empire.
Sand fizzes on the sea, wind flutters a flag
and the boat sinks to the bottom.

Neither you nor I are here anymore.

In the sky a pair of birds circles
with no place to land.

TONGUES OF BABYLON

Instead of paying, I left my hand on the counter.
The last night.
Light licked a doe.
Radio Babylon squawked out requests
for the dead riders returning from the disco.
Before the doe jumps, it freezes and her eyes shine for a moment.

— — —

I'm lying in a quiet ravine in moist, warming leaves.
I nibble lichen before I venture into the field.

The doe crosses over among the houses.
She avoids the scrap metal collectors before looking into a window
after a Friday quarrel.
She finds the right door.
She sits at the table.
She speaks kindly with my wife
and a plate shines into a human face
like a moon.

COUPLET

Two hills are immersed in a silent discussion.
A thousand intimate years between each reply.

AGAINST SLUGS

I set out glasses for slugs.
Better than killing them with the edge of a shovel.
You put into the shade the washing that has to dry slowly.
A trail from a jet intersects the laundry line.
Night evaporates off the birds.

In the heart beats a clock in a fight with a fissure.
I set aside another poem.
Reading has failed, not poetry.
The skeleton in the boy bounces upon the swing,
and when it's all the way up,
I see his eyes:
two infinitely deep holes in a skull.

* * *

The Danube in Bratislava is not wider than the Elbe in Roudnice.
The bells of the church are not heard from the house.
From the house I hear the train crossing's signal calling to mass.
Here a peacock wards off death, the rooster is dead.
A little girl rescues ladybugs from the baptismal font beneath the rain gutter.

THE LANE TO KŘEKOV

A second of thought
as I pass the lane to Křekov—

Does anyone still live here?

I've never walked it, always avoiding it:
steps click here like a revolver.

Worn walls with a heated scab—
Even here people loved each other
and dipped the whiteness of backs in black roof beams,
even before they started to rot.

Now the vapor of breath in stone.

Everything here is rusting and baring its layers.
And that second of thought softens
and twitches like a grasshopper
that leaves its hind leg
between your fingers.

MAPLE

Every year I go to the end of the garden to the maple,
which I nurtured from a tiny seedling I found,
and trim its branches.

On the scarred bark a terrified eye blinks
as, year after year,
a determined god approaches it with shears.

* * *

I gaze into the sun and I'm already someone else.
I was born in my children,
a graying Odysseus, I hold up one spotted,
dried-up hand before me like a bough.
After the pleasures of love I indulge in the pleasure of narration

about light that quivers in the door,
about a never-seen harbor
on whose shores I will finally die
with eyes inflamed by the sun like a Greek dog.

VIKING SHIELDS

I scribbled this poem on a picture of an angel.
His arms outstretched like my love for humanity.
That's you, Papa, you.
When she wants to make me happy, she calls me Papa.
The younger one comes and stands at the door
like a mischievous ghost.
He says nothing. And it's a nothing that means nothing.
My shields against emptiness.

When I finally pass into it,
they'll find me in a spring thaw with my love for humanity.
They'll recognize me from the screw in my left foot,
a medal I earned
in foot tennis.

FROM *THE SIXTH FINGER* (2022)

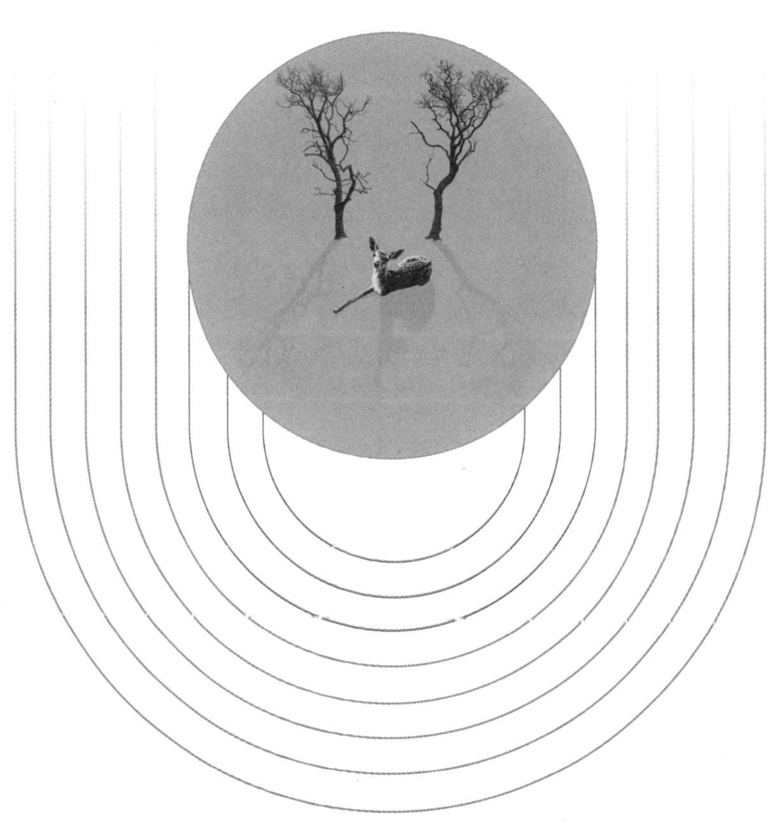

THE WELL

I lean forward until my fingers dig into the lichen
gnawing at the wellhead
I'm looking for Jewish treasure, SS ammunition, a drowned cat

I drop something in, the surface ripples

The eye of the well opens slowly
I see it looking for me, focusing, aiming

WELCOME

I.

I slow to the speed of a fingernail and can't see
how the clean dirties, the full empties
how the strong weakens and the empty fills
I throw off speed like a ballast
and don't hear it land

The heart spilled in the motorcyclist's chest
He's been brought to the ground on one knee
He leans heavily against the forest's doorstep
A red ribbon stretches between his nose and the earth
and the forest, ever indifferent,
welcomes him with an outstretched branch

II.

A little boy came across the word *infinity* for the first time
He sucks his finger into an elderly, white thumb

He stands at the forest's edge, afraid to enter the thought
where the left eye looks at the right

Here black snouts pitch baby mice up to the sky

IT'S ABOUT TIME

I.

The movement of birds indicates that spring will come again this year

It's time to place a foot into someone else's footprint and go out to the forest's edge
where the sun hunts us like vermin

It's clouding over: an airplane slips through a cloud like a zipper on a postman's pouch

It's possible we were born in a pouch

I'm not alone, there are many whose breathing is synchronized with mine at this moment

II.

If you offer me eternity
I want to be a mollusk suctioned to the weathered concrete of a pier
To soak up with the whole of my massive foot, like a brain
To listen to the world through a kiss
To live as touch

MOUNTAINS

A train whose passengers have no eyes,
confidential images flashing through their heads

Elder trees and acacias rush by the train and into the distance
like missiles fired into the past

Fields and towns are slower

Mountains flow slowest of all

NIGHT SWIMMER

A train is hauling wood, rust, and blue shipping containers to Hamburg

You plug your ears, avert your eyes, and you're half a lifetime older

The wind has removed you from your mouth
and you, mouthless, are rustling in the leaves across the river

Cormorants sleeping in the branches
will strip themselves like scabs from the tree's crown come morning

A night swimmer immerses himself in the quarry pond

He takes his first stroke and his pale wrinkled tip
flashes under the water like the embryo of a star

CRETAN NIGHT

I.

I read with my finger on paper and the finger devours the text
Suddenly it's here: mountains sail and ships loom
The sail tightens the wind and drives the sea beneath it

A city blazes above a valley and illuminates a mountain of unrest
approaching like a giant ferry

Moon like a sickle and black grass
rising beneath its blade

All things in the world are shadow, depth, and light

II.

Light wanders from the Venetian fortress
I look back and the sea shifts the whole coast

A match plows wrinkles into the face
And the hand burns

The wind tears a cough and a dark plant
disseminates a few sparks of ash
Who is it?

No one remembers us
behind the light of the fortress

III.

We stood on the cape
and watched the coastal fires

Laughter carried in from the distance, words twinkled
and lit up a mouth and part of a face

We said goodbye and walked into the dark
Only talons and feathers remained of the sun

What remained of us supported us in darkness
Women's cries fell from the cliff into the lake

IV.

In Palaiochora they will bring a pitcher full of light
and we can stay

The wind takes a wave in its mouth and spits it on Amazonia
Siberia burns and writhes like a foreign face, far away Australia burns

I'll reach out for water like a root wandering in a tomb
All of the wind will shine in my blood

The thin shirt stretches like a Greenlandic flag
into which someone coughed up something alive

I've forgotten everything but the wind

LOCKDOWN

After weeks we walked out pale and fragile
The air like a damp towel under our noses

The letters in the marble cried
and we watched the benevolent sun

After a year we walked out plump and soft
New species of insects were hatching, the graves
were steaming beyond the woods
Every Rudolph was dead

In the center of the brightest light was the greatest darkness

The branch bent but did not break

HEART OF A SHREW

Are those annoying sparrows still there?

And the fish? Do they touch the surface to taste the light?
And the mountain ranges? The ones that form silently?

Only the ones that form silently, I say

Fruit fly, laughter, kiss, poem?
The hem of a skirt wrapped around a ring finger?

Yes, yes, I say:

And the heart of a shrew? Does it still beat six hundred times a minute?

Yes, yes, I reply:
Almost six hundred times

CORRIDA DE TOROS

I.

Young men gut a truck with their hands
and dump large chunks of its innards onto the asphalt

One, the half-naked one, jumps on it like it's a bull
As he pulls a banderilla out of its neck
the muscles of his buttocks clench, hard as a fist

The mountain glitters indifferently in the evening glow
The truck exhales heavily

The soft sun heats the parts white-hot, and the hard, sharp bodies
cut the air like steel sheets

II.

Later, when I went down pensively to the river at dusk
I saw light stretch the back of a boy
trying to raise the Cathedral of the Virgin Mary's Birth
and a girl's legs embracing him and helping him with all her strength

III.

Pollen grains drift down onto the endless river

On the shore I take my hands out of my pockets
and place them on the bow of a fishing boat

I send them downstream
and watch them disappear with the boat at the bend

REARING HORSE

Snow covers dark Zalmon, yet Czech mountains are gray

At a bus stop, a man sticks his index finger through a hole in his boot
The bus arrives and opens its doors to the frost
People swarm out, rattling their poles
eyes stuck inside their heads like candies in a pocket
They carry smooth, hot hearts in their bodies

They carry to lay them in the snowdrift

—— —— ——

At the border, a calf-deep white plain
They walk single file to where the ski tracks point
Behind a thin fence a man in the snow with a fur cap
is holding, on a frostbitten rope
a horse rearing up like an Alaskan church

DOTS

They're sitting in camouflage by a dying fire
The tree behind their backs swells without light
and grain passes the wind from ear to ear
He has a weakness for her protruding incisor, leaning against her lower lip
she enjoys the sight of his skinny, sparkling thighs

They don't hear the screech of a particle
flying through space for them

AT THE END OF TOWN

I.

In the hallway of the house I was hurrying to escape
a mirror stopped me in my tracks
A strange face there; my smile hatched from it
like a frightened fish

II.

So, I walked out of the house and slowly let myself be led
My forehead glows from the text like the headlight of a bathyscaph, I head for the surface

The lamps space out and the lights of the dwellings reluctantly fade
except for the cosmic station that floats oarless through space

The night hums like it was putting us to its ear

Then nature suddenly goes silent and lays a flickering soul before me

I set it in my palm and lightly blow on it

AT NECHRANICE

My father and I take turns at the oar on the borrowed rowboat
and lowering the bait in the flooded sandpit

We drag a rain cloud behind us
and when the storm breaks, we're not ready

The wind pushes the boat from the shore against human power
my son dumps the fish and uses the bucket
to empty the boat of water

We're rowing

I don't know why I'm now thinking of a book
my place marked with a small white handkerchief

Is someone giving me the answer to a question
I haven't asked?

We're rowing, but we can't anymore

Behind that cloud
the sun is bright as a word, I know that

but the one who thinks of every move for me
I don't know

IN HOŘOVICE

Ivan Slavík was our guide through the Sun Gate
He darkly declared that the sun wrought above the gate was the shape of nothingness
It was getting dark, the statues were twisting
and the old Catholic poet wore a fish-like expression as demons visited him at night.

Did even Proteus turn into a nightingale despite his fish head?
Ivan creased a cross beneath his shirt
Whoever passes through the Sun Gate won't go mad that day

WE'RE TOGETHER AGAIN

We've been together a hundred thousand years
Jebel Sahaba Fineilspitze Wadjak
Acum Cave with the six-fingered handprint
The sun shines the same on everyone
What has been will be again

You'll recognize me by my handshake

You have a weakness for overgrown footpaths
where everything renews itself like skin
and for bark where uninviting sap oozes and dries

Don't scratch off that scab
You're drawn by sharp grass that licks ankles to the bone
An insect eating another insect's head
A thrush with a broken talon

A glacier pours back gravel from an ancient warm sea
Gravel covers the tracks of another glacier
that enclosed a trilobite lake like the diaphragm

Summer in the mountains uncovers the mummy of a hunter
From its twisted mouth I read:

I was here
like you

NOTES

"Into the Darkness"

Michele Ranchetti (Milan, 14 October 1925–Florence, 2 February 2008) was an Italian historian, translator, and poet.

"The Lane to Křekov"

Křekov is a small street in the poet's city, Roudnice nad Labem.

"Viking Shields"

Foot tennis, also known as "football tennis," "futnet," "soccer tennis," and, in Czech and Slovak, "nohejbal," is a game similar to tennis, played on a tennis court with a tennis net and only using body parts except for the hands to strike the ball.

"Rearing Horse"

Zalmon is a region or mountain mentioned in Psalm 68:14 (KJV Salmon) where God apparently scattered enemies of Israel by means of a snowstorm.

"In Hořovice"

The Sun Gate is a Baroque sun-themed gate that serves as the entrance to the park at Hořovice Chateau, Czech Republic.

ACKNOWLEDGMENTS

There is a long history of support and enthusiasm that made the publishing of this work possible.

In addition to the gratitude we feel toward the University of Pittsburgh Press, the Pitt Poetry Series, and all those who worked on this project, the poet and translator would like to express sincere thanks to Jan Zikmund for his care as both a literary agent and critical reader of our work.

We would also like to thank the literary magazine *B O D Y* for expressing early interest in publishing our work.

We thank Host Publishing in Brno, Czech Republic, for publishing the original Czech versions of these poems.

Poems from the *A Secret Life* section previously appeared in *A Secret Life* (2021), published by Blue Diode Press, Edinburgh, UK. We gratefully acknowledge Rob A. Mackenzie for granting permission to reprint these translations.

We would also like to thank the publishers and editors who saw value in our work, including it in their publications. A partial list includes *Modern Poetry in Translation*, *The Dark Horse Magazine*, *The New York Review of Books*, *Poetry London*, and *PN Review*.